CHAMPIONSHIP BOWLS

CHAMPIONSHIP BOWLS

Bill Irish

With an Introduction by David Bryant, MBE

DAVID & CHARLES
Newton Abbot   London   North Pomfret (Vt)

British Library Cataloguing in Publication Data

Irish, Bill
  Championship bowls.
    1. Bowling on the green
    I. Title
    796.31   GV909

    ISBN 0–7153–7469–9

Typeset by
Northern Phototypesetting Company, Bolton, Greater Manchester
Printed in Great Britain by
Redwood Burn Ltd, Trowbridge & Esher
for David & Charles (Publishers) Limited
Brunel House, Newton Abbot, Devon

Published in the United States of America
by David & Charles Inc
North Pomfret, Vermont 05053 USA

Contents

Introduction

by David Bryant, MBE

Having toured with Bill Irish and been a fellow member of the England team on many occasions, I can say that, even in a sport with such a high tradition as bowls, there could not be a better team man or sportsman. This does not prevent him, as his record shows, from being an especially fine Singles player with an excellent temperament.

I feel that much of his success stems from starting, as I did, very young when the muscles are loose and the joints supple. The good habits which you acquire through this early start become invaluable later.

Whenever bowlers meet socially, they invariably discuss matches from the past, either their own or ones they have seen. I am sure, therefore, that there will be great interest in the diagrams in this book which recreate specific match situations, some of which I was involved in myself.

Bowls diagrams are nothing new, of course, but there still seems to be some unexplored potential in recording notable matches for posterity. This cannot be done as comprehensively or as accurately as in chess, nor is it necessary, but it is a way of preserving some of the feel of a match beyond what is contained in the bare final result. The series of diagrams from the last few ends of my match against Bill in the final of the National Benzole Master Bowler tournament recorded by HTV helped me re-live that enjoyable match as it built up to its tense climax.

David Bryant, MBE, was World Singles champion in 1966 and Commonwealth Games Singles champion in 1962, 1970, 1974 and 1978. He has won the English Singles title six times and the British Isles title four times.

1   The Road to the Top

In a sense, I was born into bowls. The Sidemoor Bowling Club at Bromsgrove, Worcestershire – the town where I have lived all my life – belonged to my grandfather. As a very young lad I used to play there, and by the time I was ten I had my first set of woods, bought for my birthday by my father. But though that property eventually came into my possession, it is more than twenty years since I played there. Those boyhood games, which I enjoyed so much, were under the rules of the English Bowling Federation, a smaller group than either the English Bowls Association (EBA) – the level green governing body – or its crown green equivalent. Today, I play under EBA rules.

The Federation game is an individual contest with each player bowling two woods. There was a local rule in the Bromsgrove League that any wood finishing more than 4ft from the jack did not count. We played against different pubs and clubs all over the country and I won the club championship when I was twelve. Not that I had any particular ambition in bowls then: it was just a pleasant part of my life. I have played most sports: rugby, hockey and cricket at Bromsgrove School; cricket for Bromsgrove Town; table tennis in the local league; and I sprinted and long-jumped for Home Command during my National Service. In fact, during the period 1949–52 there were so many demands on my time that I was unable to play bowls regularly. But in 1952, I started again. By this time, my father had left the Federation game and joined Hewell Bowling Club, the nearest club playing under EBA rules.

I played about twice a week at first, simply for the enjoyment I got out of it, but I took a greater interest when my uncle, Eric Mansell, was made Worcestershire captain. I travelled with him to many matches, soaking up the atmosphere, picking up a few wrinkles and talking about the game. Yet as far as my style goes, it wasn't my uncle I modelled myself on, but another Hewell bowler, Ernie Green, who had an England trial in 1954.

It was in 1952 that I first played for Worcestershire, as a lead. I retired again in 1955, but in 1960 I was back, and I've continued to play for the county ever since, initially as a lead, twice at No3 and, since 1965, as a skip.

Though I would have to place international bowls at the top of the list in terms of skill and ultimate satisfaction, I prefer county bowls to all other forms of the game. Not only is it very competitive, but it gives me an opportunity almost every weekend to renew friendships I have made all over the country. It is still one of my main ambitions to play for Worcestershire in a winning Middleton Cup side; we reached the quarter-finals in 1974 and the semi-finals in 1976, but we have yet to take the trophy.

It was not until I won the Pairs with Cliff Powell at the City of Worcester August Bank Holiday Tournament in 1963 that I began to develop a real taste for competition. From then on, there was no stopping me; I entered everything I could and soon there were very few summer evenings and weekends when I was not to be found on a bowling green.

In 1965, I won both the Worcestershire Singles and the Pairs (with Cliff Powell) which meant that I qualified for the EBA Championships at Mortlake. I lost in the first round but, rather like a tennis player must feel about Wimbledon, it was obvious to me that these championships had a special quality and atmosphere. I didn't feel particularly bad about losing but my first visit certainly stimulated the desire to play there again.

A national title is difficult to win in any sport but an added difficulty peculiar to bowls arises from the sheer weight of numbers entering. The four events – Singles, Pairs, Triples and Rinks – attract a combined entry of over seventy thousand. These numbers are whittled down by county Championships, which are played on a home or away basis, and it is no joke for an international to be drawn away to a supposedly inferior player on a green with peculiarities known only to those who play on it regularly.

The ability to read strange greens and adapt to them is invaluable in these circumstances. I have come to realise that this is perhaps one of my stronger points because, looking back, I can't remember ever having lost to someone who I may privately have considered to be a mediocre performer. This may be because I enjoy the challenge of coping with various conditions in all sorts of weather. It's a lovely feeling to have the sun on your back, but I enjoy playing even if it's raining or blustery. Perhaps this is why I've never really taken to indoor bowls, though I do play once or twice a week through the winter at Worcester. I can enjoy a match indoors and it's good for keeping in touch with my bowling friends, but the artificial enclosed atmosphere and the lack of variety in the running of the greens make it, for me, a very poor second to the outdoor game. I wouldn't like to go through the whole winter without playing at all, but it would bore me to distraction to play as much indoors in the winter as I do outdoors in the summer.

In 1967 I made a change which turned out to be the best decision I ever made. I joined the Vines Park Bowling Club at Droitwich, where the general standard was high and – more to the point – very competitive. I won the EBA Singles during my first year as a member there, and if I hadn't joined the club, I don't think I would have won it. I went down to Mortlake with a completely open mind. Nobody expected anything special from me. I didn't myself; I just played each match as it came, and it wasn't until I beat Ray Moore (Cumberland) 21–18 after 26 ends in the quarter-finals that I thought I had a chance. I can remember thinking then that even if I got no further, at least I would have a medal to show for my efforts.

My semi-final against Harold Jepson from Redcar was very close all through and twice I had to save the match, until a single on the last end gave me victory 21–20 and put me through to the final against Fred Horn, a former England captain from Torquay. He led me 12–9 but, partly through making him bowl a series of full-length jacks and partly because as the younger man I was still fresh and keen when he started to falter, I went on to win 21–12.

As English champion I played in the British Isles Championships at Belmont, Northern Ireland, where I lost 21–7 in the final to Roy Fulton, the Northern Ireland champion.

People outside bowls might be surprised that my achievements did not automatically put me in the England team. I had an England trial in 1966, and another in 1968, but although I became an indoor international in that year I wasn't selected for the England outdoor team until I won the EBA Singles for the second time in 1974.

It is often unfair to displace the man in possession. With Rink play, the selectors also have to consider blends and combinations. Even so, winning the EBA Singles did change a few things. Bowls is a quiet game and perhaps because most bowlers are of mature years, the game doesn't produce 'stars' in the way other sports do. The media, too, give the game relatively little coverage, and there is no fear of becoming a national celebrity overnight. But I did receive some nice local publicity and many invitations to bowls dinners to display the cup. One of the pleasant aspects of bowls is that if you have a big win, by and large the people you play with through the year share your pleasure, and your relationship with them remains the same. I hope this will always be the case.

There is no doubt that winning my first national championship made bowls more important to me. It gave me the mental breakthrough of knowing I could win at top level. It gave me a standard to live up to in my own mind and a certain standing in the game which made other bowlers keener to beat me. Playing a national champion was a special challenge to my opponents which got their adrenalin going and most of them raised their games when they played me. I can't say that winning taught me anything about the technique of the game that I didn't already know, but it did help to fix certain good match-playing habits in my mind. I learnt to concentrate, not to rush – and the importance of consistency.

For the next few years, I continued to play for Vines Park, Worcestershire and in tournaments with a fair measure of success without landing anything big, with the exception of the Denny

Cup – the National Indoor Two-Rink Championship – which Vines Park won in 1970. As we had only twenty-one indoor members, we were the smallest club in the competition but we had a great team spirit.

In 1974, just after I won the Worcestershire Singles, my mother died. My father was very upset and in an attempt to cheer him up I said: 'Come with me to Worthing and I'll win the Singles for you.'

In contrast to my previous visits, I actually went with the intention of winning it. Very determined, I played well – and none of my opponents scored more than 14 shots! It was, incidentally, the first final ever to be televised by the BBC, but to me this was infinitely less important than the pleasure it gave my father. I really felt that I had won this one for him.

An exciting thought, once it had sunk in, was that only four other bowlers had ever won the championship more than once. This may have been in the England selectors' minds, too, when, after my third trial in June 1975, an international badge came my way. I played No3 in a Rink skipped by Reg Payne and we won three out of three in the 1975 home international series.

Because of the political situation, Northern Ireland could not stage the British Isles Championships in 1974, but I had my chance in 1975 at Llanelli when, in very wintry conditions, I beat John Fleming, the Scottish champion, 21–17 in the final. This led to the great thrill of my being selected for England's squad of five for the 1976 World Championships in Johannesburg. In little more than twelve months I had progressed from being just a county player to what was considered to be one of England's five best players.

Our other four players – David Bryant, Tom Armstrong, John Evans and Peter Line – were all more experienced than I, but I don't think any of them had visualised the magnificent way in which the event was staged. The hospitality and every aspect of the arrangements were first class, the greens were as true as any I've ever played on – and to play in a bowls match watched by ten thousand people was something I had never even considered. It certainly indicated what the potential of the game might be.

13

The South Africans were outstanding. Doug Watson won the Singles and they won the Pairs, Triples and Rinks as well. With Bryant as lead, myself at No2 and Armstrong as skip, we took the silver in the Triples and with Evans as lead, myself at No2, Armstrong at No3 and Line as skip we took bronze in the Fours. As a result, Bryant and I were invited to play in a Masters' Pairs tournament in Newcastle, just outside Sydney, Australia. Again, we had a great time, but unfortunately, we finished well down the field as neither of us really adjusted to the greens, which took far more bias than we were used to.

Trips like these, and a special television tournament on HTV Wales, convinced me that bowls was going to develop out of all recognition in the next decade, though I would still like to see the game receive more national press and television coverage.

Sponsorship, too, has come to bowls in a small way, and I can see the time rapidly approaching when there will be sponsored Masters' tournaments at major coastal resorts which could attract big crowds and make interesting television. To make bowls more of a spectator and television sport, large coloured discs could be used to identify the bowls, and players could wear different coloured shirts. Some of the traditionalists would be horrified, but I am sure it could be done in a tasteful way. I would not be in favour of anything which might spoil the game's character and tradition, but I believe that it is still possible to avoid this, yet move with the times.

Whether these things come to pass or not, I'm sure I shall always enjoy playing, but there is no denying that new developments in any sport are stimulating, not only to those immediately affected but to the sport as a whole.

2 Learning the Game

Anyone who would like to play bowls has only to go along to a local green and watch awhile from the bank. Get into conversation with almost any bowler, and provided it is not a deadly serious match, he will help you to get started.

You will be able to borrow a pair of soft-soled bowls shoes (or even make do with a pair of pumps) and a set of woods. After a few games, there won't be any great difficulty in joining a club; you will then want to buy your own shoes and woods – though before you buy woods you should experiment a little to find a set which suits you and which feels good in the hand. I use Henselite simply because I prefer the feel to that of any other, though there are, of course, many players who feel exactly the opposite. A bowl may vary between $4\frac{1}{4}$in and $5\frac{1}{8}$in in diameter and I would advise using the largest size with which you can feel comfortable. A wood which is too small tends to slip out of the hand.

The expense of kitting yourself out completely with white flannels, waterproofs and accessories isn't necessary until you are well on the way to playing competitively.

Formal coaching has become available only comparatively recently but the EBA coaching scheme has taken root in most counties to such an extent that almost every club possesses it own coach. It has also become accepted that bowls is no longer an 'old man's game' – if it ever was. If any non-bowling friend makes this remark to me, I simply invite him to have a game. After an afternoon's bending and stretching I guarantee that he will feel a bit stiff the next morning unless he is unusually fit.

In general, more and more young people are playing bowls and a few schools have even introduced the game to some of their sixth-form pupils. The EBA does not accept entries for its national championships from players under sixteen, but as I go round the clubs I see many bowlers younger than this who already display a good grasp of the basic skills.

Bowls is a simple game. Unlike some other games – tennis, for instance, where strokes like the service and backhand are quite difficult to master – bowls is a game at which almost anyone can soon achieve a good enough standard to enjoy playing.

The basic game is easy to grasp. In Singles, the player who wins the toss bowls the jack – a white ball not much bigger that a white snooker ball – to the other end of the green; or, if he so wishes, he may give it away, so that he has last bowl. Whether he bowls it short or long is up to him provided that it travels at least 25yd and is at least 6ft from the opposite ditch. Then, bowling alternately, each player delivers four woods. The player whose wood finishes nearest the jack scores one. If his second wood is nearer than his opponent's nearest, he scores two and so on. The winner of a particular 'end' bowls the jack for the next end. This can be an important tactical advantage. In Pairs, each player delivers four woods; in Triples three and in Rinks (or Fours) two.

The most fundamental aspect of bowls is to 'draw' to the jack – that is, to leave your wood as near as possible to it. You need a good sense of weight or strength but, more important, you will need to be able to judge precisely how much your wood will curve as it travels up the green. A bowl is not round, but elliptical. This gives it 'bias' so that it travels in the sort of arc shown in Figure 1. It is possible to regulate the degree of bias either by a small variation in the grip or by the speed at which the wood is bowled. The faster the delivery, the less the bias will operate.

Other factors have to be reckoned with, too. Greens vary in the amount of bias and weight they take, and the same green will play differently at different times of year. In early summer, greens will tend to be slow and heavy and the arc a wood will take will be much narrower than after several weeks of hot weather.

On a fast green, a wood travelling slowly will take much longer to stop completely than it will on a slow green. This gives a player a much better chance of squeezing woods in at a sharp angle when the road to the jack appears to be blocked.

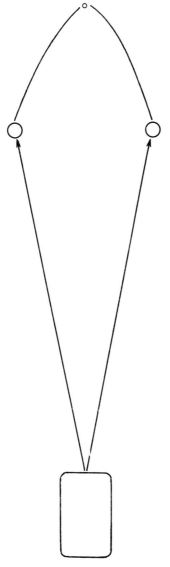

Fig 1

In Britain, except after a prolonged spell of hot weather, it will be uncommon for a green to run at more than 15 seconds timed over 30yd. I have known greens run as slowly as 9 seconds. In Australia and New Zealand you will regularly bowl on greens of 18 seconds. In Australia they rarely run at less than 13 seconds and in New Zealand they often run at 22, or as much as 26, seconds.

On a slow, heavy green, the arc is relatively narrow. The path to the jack is thus more easily blocked. One green may take a wider arc on the backhand (that is, for a right-hander, when the wood pulls into the jack from the left) than it does on the forehand with the wood pulling in from the right. From the opposite end, the reverse will be true. As a green dries out, or when the atmosphere becomes overcast and humid, its behaviour will also change.

All these variations have to be sized up as quickly as possible. So too do the variations within the players' control. The player who wins the toss or who, by winning the previous end, earns the option of where he places the mat (not less than 4ft from the back ditch or 27yd from the front ditch, except the first end when it is placed 4ft in) has a tactical advantage. He can choose to bowl either a long or short jack and either give himself the chance to bowl to the length that he prefers and/or make his opponent bowl to a length which he would not choose himself. It is, for instance, common for veterans – even very good players – to find it harder to bowl to long jacks simply because their natural strength and co-ordination is not what it used to be. Conversely there are some bowlers who are heavy-handed and who do not possess the smoothness and delicacy of touch which is called for in the short game. Many of these 'up-and-at-it' bowlers with a robust style are capable of giving me a good game if all the jacks are long, therefore, I get them on short jacks at the earliest opportunity.

At the commencement of any end, the aim of each player will always be to draw as close to the jack as he can, but once a cluster of woods – known as a 'head' – starts to develop, other types of shots may be employed. There is, for instance, the 'trail'. In Figure 2

18

Fig 2

Player O stands three shots to the good. It might be possible for Player X to draw even closer to the jack than O's woods but the chances are against it. Even if X was successful, he would score only one and with O still having his fourth and last wood to come X could not be certain of holding out even this one shot advantage.

However, if X can make his last wood hit the jack firmly enough to send it through, as the Figure shows, to two of his other woods at the back of the green, he can turn a deficit of three into an advantage of two – possibly three if his fourth wood comes through far enough. Furthermore, O now has a difficult task with his final wood.

The 'yard-on' is so-called because the intention is to shift an opposing wood a yard or so on while one's own wood remains in the same position. More rarely, a yard-on would be played with the object of contacting one of one's own short woods to play it into the head.

In Figure 3, for instance, it would be a mistake to use too much pace because you might not only take out the intended wood but perhaps some of your own woods as well. On the other hand, if you make contact as shown at just the right weight, your own wood should remain within an inch or so of the position the opposing wood was occupying, thus leaving you holding as many as three shots.

The yard-on can also be used to nudge a previous wood into a better position though you would never do this if there was room to get the wood you are bowling in to the jack direct. In other words, it is easier to do this with one wood by means of a draw than with two.

Because of the speed at which it is played, the 'take out' is usually less predictable (Figure 4). Unlike the draw or yard-on, the take out requires the bowler to allow very little for the bias. This is simply because the wood is bowled at much greater speed so it will not have had time to turn over on its side as the bias comes into operation and trace out its normal arc by the time it reaches the head.

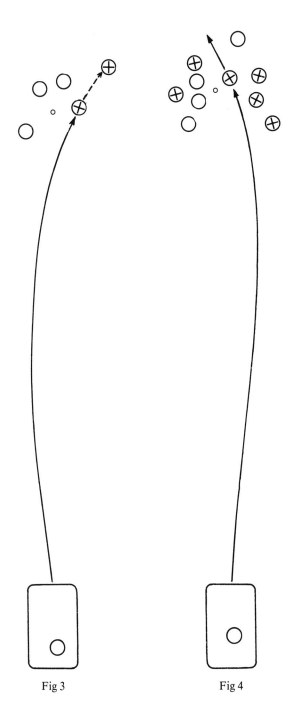

Fig 3

Fig 4

Therefore, allowing no bias on fast greens and very little on greens of ordinary-to-slow pace, your object is simply to remove at least some of your opponent's scoring woods. Your own wood will almost certainly be travelling too fast to remain in a scoring position but, hopefully, some of the woods you have previously bowled will now score.

The 'firing' shot operates on the same principle as the take out but there is more of an element of last-ditch desperation to it. It is bowled with maximum controllable force and its object is simply to destroy an otherwise impregnable, or nearly impregnable, position. It requires skill in aiming but even more it requires a strong element of luck, for in scattering woods and jack far and wide it is impossible to predict where they will finish.

In general, though, the golden rule is: never fire unless there is no reasonable alternative. It is not only unpredictable but, in my opinion, a little at odds with the essential character of the game. Bowls is, after all, a quiet game of touch, skill, thought and tactics. Anyone who made a habit of firing, end after end, would not only make himself unpopular with the green committee but would, with such an emphasis on brute force and chance, spoil the enjoyment of those attempting to play properly.

That is not to say that firing is not part of the game; it is. When the situation demands, I fire without any compunction whatsoever. However, he who fires is always at a temporary psychological disadvantage because he is admitting that his opponent has been too skilful for him on this particular end.

A few days before I wrote this, my rink was leading by nine shots in an EBA County Fours quarter-final when, with my last wood of the end, I faced a deficit of five. I could have fired and, with the head as it was, could hardly have made matters worse. The odds were very much against me drawing the shot, but when I managed to do so the psychological effect was tremendous.

Our opponents, feeling themselves certain to recover to only four behind and thus get well back in the match, were completely shattered when their deficit went from nine to ten. They must have felt that after that there was no way they could ever recover. For our part, having averted the threat of having our lead drastically reduced, we felt there was no way we could lose, provided that we kept our heads.

If, however, we had been in arrears by the same margin on that occasion, I would almost certainly have fired. Nine shots in arrears will inevitably have dented one's confidence and this will tend to make a difficult shot appear even more difficult.

When shots down, one mental attitude I try to cultivate when skipping is to convince myself that I am shots up, especially when I am playing the draw. If I think of myself as drawing for an extra shot, I will invariably save, probably by drawing second or third shot. If I think that all I've got to do is draw another shot, the position will invariably look easier.

This illustrates another important point: bowlers are human beings who may feel better or worse or more or less confident on different days, often for no apparent reason. Be aware of how you are feeling and play to your limitations. If you are feeling good, don't be afraid to be a little more ambitious.

Apart from the draw, the trail, the yard-on, the take-out and the fire, the keen newcomer to bowls will come to appreciate the value of the 'block' and the infinite variety of 'cannons' or 'wicks' which may occur when woods are closely grouped.

The block, as its name implies, is a defensive type of shot – seldom used and difficult to execute – intended to protect winning position. In Figure 5, for instance, player X holds two shots. He has little prospect, by drawing to the jack, of improving his position. Player O, if he is allowed a clear path, could attempt to come in on the back hand hoping to nudge his front wood either in on the jack or to cannon X's shot wood away. Alternatively, he might elect to fire. However, if X places his last wood into a blocking position, O will be unable to do either.

Many cannons or wicks occur simply by chance, but it is sometimes possible, if the head lies in a certain way, to bowl a wood with the intention of flicking off the edge of another to finish in a scoring position. Figure 6 illustrates the position where there is no other way of depriving one's opponent of the shot.

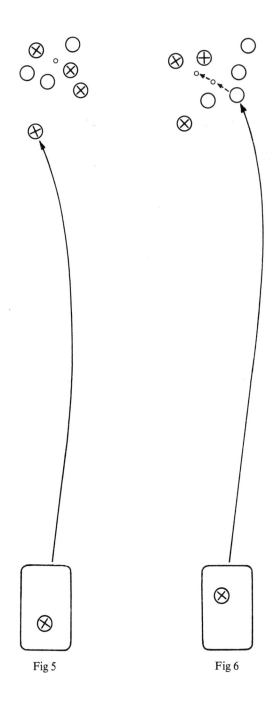

Fig 5

Fig 6

A wick is a convenient term for a thin contact with another wood or woods. There is plenty of scope for lucky or unlucky wicks when a wood may glance off one, two, three or even four other woods, but heads do present themselves when a wick may be the only way to get the shot. In Figure 6, for instance, X is three shots down. He can transform the situation by playing for a wick off the right-hand of O's two front woods. If he judges this right, he has every prospect of trailing the jack through for three.

3 The Right Approach

Plate 1

Plate 2

The Grip

There are three basic ways in which a bowler may grip his wood – by using the 'cradle', the 'claw' or the 'finger' grips.

The cradle is probably the most natural – and the most popular – grip. It is used by some 90 per cent of the bowlers I know, but I don't use this grip myself. Many users of the cradle grip are very good players, and I would be the last to suggest there is anything wrong with it. But the golden rule is to adopt the method that suits you best, and it is for this reason that I prefer the claw. The finger grip has generally agreed disadvantages and is best avoided.

As its name implies, the cradle grip is formed simply by using your four fingers as the cradle and lining your thumb directly along the side of the bowl to keep it stable in your hand. As Plate 1 (forehand) and Plate 2 (backhand) show, the bowl fits snugly into the hand with the fingers, as shown by the frontal view of Plate 3,

Plate 3

quite close together. The two middle fingers are slightly closer together than the others. Most bowlers start with this grip and never see any reason to change.

With the claw (Plates 4–6), the two middle fingers stay close together but the forefinger and little finger are spread out much more widely than with the cradle. The thumb sticks up 2in or so at about a 45-degree angle. I believe that this gives me more control. I am gripping a wider area of the bowl than I would with the cradle, and with the claw, my span is about 5in, compared with 4in for the cradle. This gives me a great deal more *feel*.

The position of the thumb has an additional value in that I use it for sighting, for lining up the shot and for aiming. Without the thumb, there would be just the rounded surface of the bowl and it is correspondingly more difficult to judge your line. In fact if you want to use your thumb to help you aim, you must use the claw because it is just too uncomfortable to stick your thumb up at an angle and keep all your fingers underneath.

Plate 4

Plate 5

Plate 6

Plate 7

Plate 8

Despite all these theoretical advantages of the claw, don't use it if you feel perfectly happy with the cradle. I can only say from my own experience that with the cradle I tend to pull my woods and therefore undergreen them.

The finger grip (Plate 7) is obviously much more unsteady than either the cradle or the claw. The bowl is supported precariously by the fingers alone without any assistance from the palm. In the actual bowling action, only the bottoms of the fingers are used, so it is impossible to generate the power that is readily available with the cradle or claw, in both of which the palm of the hand goes into the delivery and can generate any weight that is required. One could get away with the finger grip on very fast or indoor greens, but most greens in Britain are heavy for much of the season so my advice is to forget about it.

You will notice from some of the pictures in this chapter that I carry a rag in my non-bowling (left) hand. My fingers tend to sweat, and when I come to the mat I like them to be not exactly bone dry but reasonably dry. The bowl can also pick up moisture from the atmosphere or the green and one way or another, it is only too easy for a wood to slip out of your hand. This is why, in any game or match I play, I wipe every wood I pick up to bowl and I wipe my fingers every time I come to the mat. I have always done this, and now do so automatically.

Plate 8 shows how I change my grip for firing shots, bringing my thumb right to the top of the bowl as an aid to sighting.

The Delivery

There are two basic forms of delivery: the upright and the crouch. The upright method is by far the more popular and many excellent bowlers use it, but I prefer the crouch.

The point at which you actually release the bowl is the same whichever method you use, so we shall discuss the different ways in which a bowler can arrive at that release point.

As the Plate sequences 9–12, 13–15 show, the upright delivery consists basically of a step forward from the mat at the same time

Plate 9

Plate 10

Plate 11

Plate 12

Plate 13

Plate 14

Plate 15

as your bowling arm goes back. You start upright, as shown in Plates 9 and 13, taking your aim and generally getting your intentions straight in your mind. Plate 10 shows me stooping slightly from the waist prior to placing my left leg forward and taking my right arm back.

If you use the upright stance, you will develop a rhythm which will enable you to synchronise the movement of your arm and foot, but there is always the danger, particularly in moments of tension, that your action will lose the perfect co-ordination of hand and foot it may possess at its best.

Can anyone guarantee that he will put his front foot down in exactly the same place – to the inch – every time? But if he overstrides or understrides, some of the rhythm of his delivery will be lost, unless by some miracle the backswing of his arm is compensatingly shorter or longer.

I am put off the upright stance because all parts of the body are moving. Natural rhythm and timing can achieve a great deal, but my feeling remains that there is more to go wrong with the upright style than with the crouch.

With the crouch, there is no reason why you should not place your front foot exactly where you want it every time; you have, after all, all the time in the world to do so. And once you have placed your front foot, only your arm then moves and your arm is therefore all you have to worry about.

Let's go through the picture sequences on the crouch (Plates 16–19, front view and 20–23, side view).

Plates 16 and 20 show me standing on the mat not quite square. I am standing, in fact, on the line I am going to take – in this case, the forehand. My feet are pointing along the line the bowl is initially going to take. Many bowlers stand square on and bowl across their body – that is, with their arms at a slightly unnatural angle to their bodies. Few of these reach a reasonable standard and many of them eventually suffer from troublesome backs.

As I grip the bowl initially, I steady it also with my left hand – my non-bowling hand – as part of the process of making sure that I am perfectly balanced. By now, I will have decided exactly what

Plate 16

Plate 17

Plate 18

Plate 19

Plate 20

Plate 21

Plate 22

Plate 23

I'm going to do. It is fatal to start your delivery with your mind still buzzing with pros and cons and conflicting possibilities, because you will inevitably end up with a mediocre shot which is neither one thing nor the other. If you do find yourself getting down without having made your mind up, get up and start again.

Next, I place my front foot exactly where I want it, rest the bowl on the ground for a second (Plates 17 and 21) and then take it back for my backswing (Plates 18 and 22).

My front foot is comfortably placed and the side view sequence illustrates particularly well how my front leg is perpendicular from knee to ankle to give maximum stability. If my left arm was waving about somewhere, it could unbalance me so I have it tucked away nicely, resting on my left thigh.

There is not only a straight line from knee to ankle, but also from the shoulder to the fingers of my bowling arm.

As I take my arm back and bring it through (Plates 19 and 23) to the point of release and past it to complete a smooth follow-through along the line of the shot, my front leg and left arm remain still while other movement is kept to an absolute minimum. It is inevitable that the hand and body should rise slightly as the bowl reaches the back of the backswing. This does not matter, but any wobble or side-to-side movement does.

At the point of release, my hand is still low. The ideal height for the head is at a position which enables you to release the bowl with the pendulum of your swing as low as possible. The lower the trajectory at which the bowl is travelling in your hand as it reaches the point of release, the less risk there is of 'bumping'. In extreme cases − say a bowler with a troublesome back − I have seen woods released with the hand several inches from the ground. This not only does the green no good, but the odds are stacked against accuracy or control.

The crouch throws more strain on the body than the upright does, particularly to the knees and back, because you remain down on the shot for several seconds. It was for this reason that a friend of mine recently switched from crouch to upright. Fair enough. There's no enjoyment in the game if you're uncomfortable. But there is no doubt in my mind that the crouch is likely to yield better results.

There are, of course, innumerable variations on these two basic styles. Indeed, in a sense, there are as many styles as there are bowlers, and various idiosyncrasies which come to mind. In Plate 24, for instance, I am demonstrating the way David Bryant, who has won the Commonwealth Games, World, British and EBA titles, initially lines up a shot. It seems to work very well for him for no-one can argue with his record, but, for me, this movement would be superfluous to the way I initially line up my shot in Plates 16, 17, 20, and 21.

When all is said and done, everything depends – assuming aim, strength and selection of shot is right – on swinging your arm straight through two feet or so to the point of release and for a foot or so beyond it on the follow through. Everything else – balance, position of feet, keeping the head still – are means to that end.

Plate 24

Forehand and backhand

All the pictures in this section have been of a forehand draw, not for any particular reason, because you are just as likely to be bowling backhand as forehand. The delivery is, of course, the same for both forehand and backhand but, for the sake of completeness, Plates 25 (forehand) and 26 (backhand) show such differences as the angle at which one places the feet to the mat. Note in both cases, though, how my eyes are fixed firmly on the top of the arc I am intending to bowl.

Firing shots

Whether one prefers the crouch or the upright stance for all shots of ordinary strength, firing shots — simply because they do require so much extra power — demand a special technique.

Plate 25   Plate 26

Plate 27

Plate 28

Plate 29

Plate 30

Plate 31

Plate 32

Plate 33

It is impossible to deliver a firing shot from a fixed crouch position. To generate the power required, not only the momentum of a delivery stride is needed, but the longest possible backswing and room for a considerable follow-through.

Allowing nothing for the bias, because it won't have time to operate, I take aim (see Plates 27–30 and 31–33) with my feet square on the mat. Taking aim through my thumb on the top of the bowl, I step straight and take my bowling arm straight back.

With my eyes fixed firmly on the target, my right arm, which does not bend at all, then comes straight through. (It was very satisfying for me to observe from these pictures just how straight my arm does come through.)

The wood is delivered at speed, though always with a controlled action which avoids bumping it, and the vigour of the follow-through means that the back foot will leave the mat. Note, though, that even when it does, it remains over the mat (to comply with the footfault rule) and that I am perfectly balanced on my left leg.

4 Match Play Tactics

There is more than one school of thought as to which position in a Rink the novice should play. Some think that he is most effectively 'hidden' at No2 or even No3, but I would always place a beginner at lead. In fact, he should play there for at least a season and probably more.

Lead is the position in which the novice will learn most rapidly. He will learn how to bowl the jack long or short, simply from the skip instructing him in this respect.

Then, with the two woods he has, he will draw to the jack as best he can. If he can drop his woods somewhere near the jack, he has made a positive contribution to his team. This will make him feel good, will allow him to enjoy the game more, and will build his confidence. On the other hand, if his two woods are wayward, then at least there is time for his colleagues to rescue the position.

The counter argument to this is that it is so important to 'get in the head' first – that is, seize the initiative by getting your first two woods closer to the jack than your opponents' – that it is better to have an experienced lead and your novice at No2.

This is all right if everything goes according to plan – but what if your lead doesn't get in the head? You can hardly expect your novice to succeed where your experienced man has failed, so your No3 and skip will find themselves carrying too much responsibility. The chances are that they won't be able to recover from the poor start.

The No2 should, in fact, be the kingpin. He should have command of all the shots – draw, yard-on, fire – the lot, even though he will fire only rarely. So, too, should the No3, but his role will usually be either one of consolidation or of starting to reverse an adverse position which has developed, perhaps by opening up a tightly congested head which is lying against his side to give his skip at least a reasonable chance with his two woods.

The skip is there to organise and advise, draw more shots if he can, get out of trouble if he can't. It is the aspect of bowls which has come to fascinate me most. I love all forms of the game, and there is something especially satisfying about Singles because, after all, if you win you have done it entirely on your own. But, more than a third EBA Singles title, I would love to skip the EBA Fours champions.

Fours is the most complex form of the game, not only because there are sixteen woods involved but because of the infinitely variable human elements present in the eight bowlers. The good skip has to concern himself not only with his own form and technical advice but also with the subtler problem of getting the best out of his men. I always like to have had a few words with the other members of the Four a few days before an important match. We may not say anything very significant and we will certainly not attempt an excessive degree of pre-planning; but what we will do is focus our minds on the match and, in a small way, get ourselves mentally keyed up. The other chap may be preoccupied with some aspect or other of life's inevitable pressures – business, domestic or whatever – but just a few words will make the match become more of a reality in his mind. It will increase his keenness to win, if only because he will realise that you are keen to win and he doesn't want to let you down.

Even in friendly inter-club matches, or in practice roll-ups, I invariably skip, but there are times, for a change, when I would like to play at No3, No2, or even lead – not just for relaxation and something different, but to play a different sort of game. When you always play skip, you are invariably bowling into very congested heads. It demands precision, but it is different from bowling the open draw shots which are the basis of Singles.

I used to be very strongly convinced that skipping too many Fours affected my Singles. Except on the very rare occasions when I might take a morning or afternoon off work, I never play Singles except in a match. When you consider that there are also Pairs, Triples and Fours events and that all county matches and inter-club matches, and almost all friendly roll-ups, are Fours, the chances are that less than five per cent of my bowling hours are devoted to Singles.

Experience has probably helped me adjust better than I used to but, as there is no short cut to achieving this, I recommend some spells of solo practice. I used to do this a great deal and found that there was nothing like it for working on those parts of my game that I felt could be stronger.

Practice

You can never have enough practice. If you love the game, as I do, you will never find this a chore. Of course, there is a feeling of anti-climax after playing in something like the EBA Championships and then coming home to take part in an ordinary club game, but once I get on the green any feeling of anti-climax is gone within a few minutes. Perhaps this is something to do with the fellowship of bowls: as soon as you're on the green, you're among friends. And that can never be bad.

I used to go out to the green with two sets of woods and two jacks. I would set one jack long at 36yd or thereabouts and one short at 27yd and draw alternately to each. I would also place a handkerchief at the end to which I was bowling and see how many woods I could drop on to it.

I would vary this by placing a wood by the jack, and then try to take it out. I would then go on to a few firing shots. These intensive solo sessions – I went out by myself two or three times a week at one point – not only improved my touch and consistency, but enabled me to find out things which would otherwise have taken years to occur to me. When you are practising on your own, there is nothing to distract you: no conversation, no concern about winning a particular end.

It sounds like a chore, but I was so keen that I never used to find it so. This kind of practice, I believe, is of maximum value when your game is still developing. It's not everybody's cup of tea and there are some very good bowlers who have never gone out on the green on their own in their lives, but if you can buckle down to it – and still enjoy it – it would be surprising if your game didn't benefit from it.

Whether you practise by yourself or not, play as much as you can. Just as a runner trains by running, a bowler trains by bowling. This is the only way to groove your action and develop touch and consistency.

Once on the green, everybody does his best – but unless there has been some kind of mental preparation, touch and form can be elusive. Whenever I have an important match within reasonable distance of home, I try to finish work early enough to relax completely for at least an hour or, better still, two hours before I go out to play. There is nothing worse than having to rush or having your thoughts dominated by the day's pressures. Sometimes this may be unavoidable, but it's only common sense to try to minimise it when you can. The longer the journey, the less advisable it is to leap straight out of the car and on to the green.

Psychologically, the journey to a match can also be an important time. The chances are you'll all be travelling in the same car, mindful of the match, but not dwelling on it too much because gossip, jokes and general conversation all help to get your companions in a relaxed frame of mind. Anything that breaks down tension is good. Providing you have not made the fatal error of underestimating the opposition, you will find that as you step on the green, or just beforehand, your mind will focus keenly on the task in hand.

The best Fours are invariably those who get on well together off the green as well as on. If you can stand pressure together, want to win for each other as well as for yourself, and, in the last resort, can lose together without recriminations, there is nothing much wrong with your morale. The importance of team spirit may be a cliché, but like a lot of clichés it happens to be true.

Another maxim which is just as true is that one should be a good loser. I hope bowls never sees the bad temper and win-at-all-costs attitude which has marred other games. I do not think it will, because the traditional courtesy and good fellowship of the game

46

is so deeply ingrained. However, I must confess that I do not make a practice of encouraging my opponents. I will say 'well bowled' as sincerely as anyone as I shake hands with someone who has just beaten me, but until the last end has been concluded I am bowling to win and concentrating as hard as I can to that purpose. If I find myself constantly praising the opposition, it is not long before the thought creeps into my mind that they could be too good for me (or us), or that as they are bowling so well, I (or we) have no right to beat them. For me, giving too much praise to the opposition can weaken my determination – only slightly, maybe, but enough. Some bowlers are quick to praise the opposition and there are a few who can do so without any apparent ill-effect to their own form. I suppose in the end it boils down to what does or does not affect your concentration.

The novice, average club-standard bowler or improving bowler can learn a tremendous amount from a good skip. The skip can, of course, only advise: he can't bowl the wood for them. But he can, by sizing up his man's ability, his form on that particular day, his state of nerves or otherwise, call for the kind of shot that is within his ability and range, and, of course, likely to prove of some use.

There is little the skip can tell his lead, who is well aware that his job is to draw his two woods as close to the jack as he can. A few inches directly in front of the jack is ideal; a few inches diagonally to the side is good, whether at front or back; right alongside the jack is not very good as wood and jack together provide too wide a target either to trail the jack through or take the wood out. It is much better for a lead to be long rather than short. All woods at the back of the green are potentially scoring woods as there are innumerable ways in which the jack may be carried on to them.

The skip offers his lead praise and encouragement, but will not make any tactical decisions until his No2 comes to the mat. In Figure 7, I am skipping X's rink. We have had the worst of the opening exchanges as O's rink lies two shots to the good. In this situation, I would ask my No2 to just overdraw to the shot wood.

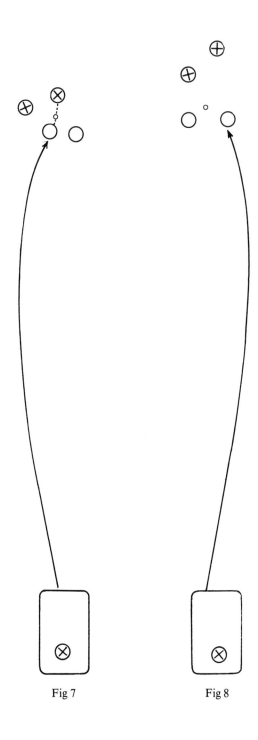

Fig 7   Fig 8

If he catches it perfectly, as shown, he will send the jack through to our back wood for shot, probably two shots. If he slightly undergreens – that is, if his wood curves across the head too soon – he will nudge out O's second wood not only to take second shot but to leave, in all probability, this wood blocking the opposition's straightforward forehand draw to the jack. If he slightly overgreens –that is, allows too much green so that the wood curves in behind the head – then it will follow through and stop some 3 or 4ft diagonally behind the jack. This is still a useful wood as it strengthens our 'behind the head' position.

In Figure 8 X's No2 again comes to the mat two shots to the bad but this initial disadvantage is not all that serious, for X's woods are both behind the jack while O's, near to the jack as they are, are short. Skipping X's rink, I would ask my No2 for a yard-on, contacting O's right-hand wood full in the face and staying there for shot or second shot. If he undergreens, he will take out O's shot wood and stay for shot. And if by some chance his wood shaves just past both O's woods, he will trail the jack into our nearest back wood for two. Barring a very poor wood, the worst that can happen is unlikely to be very bad.

By the time the No3s come to the mat, the situation usually looks more complex. The more experienced skips will by now be concentrating not only on the immediate shot in hand, but also on possible future developments. For instance, in Figure 9 O holds two shots. At first sight, the obvious course is to play either the straightforward draw on the forehand or draw off the jack high wood. But even a near-perfect shot will gain an advantage for only one, so X's skip should be bearing in mind O's lack of position at the back. Because of this, O can only draw. Therefore X can deliver a much more telling wood by attempting to trail the jack through for a likely four. If X misses the jack and hits O's shot wood, he will stop for shot.

In Figure 10, the head is so tight that X has no chance of negating O's advantage except by opening the head to give his skip a chance. X's skip should therefore call for a firing shot on to one of O's front woods. At best, the jack could be trailed through

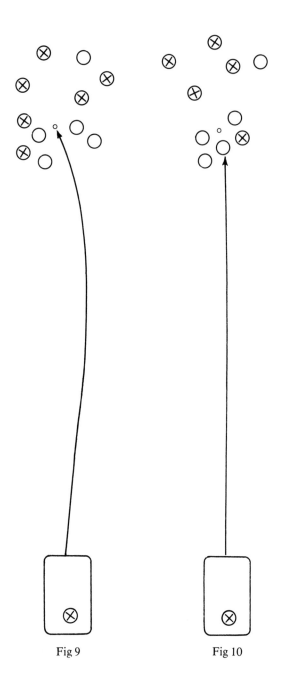

Fig 9   Fig 10

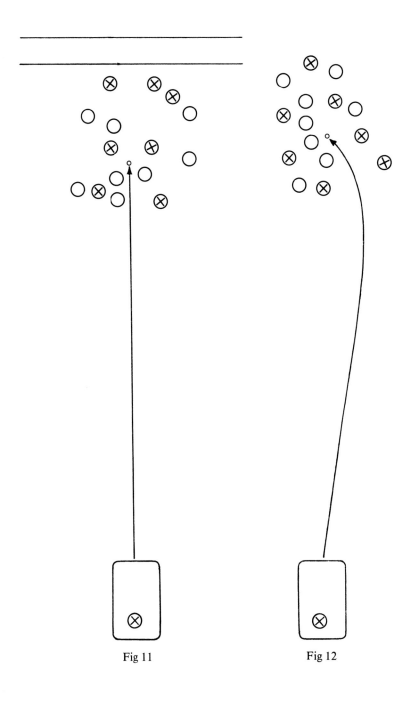

Fig 11   Fig 12

to one of X's back woods; at worst, it will open the head up and give his skip a chance.

Most complex of all, of course, are the situations which the skip himself will face.

In Figure 11, for instance, he is two shots down but has the three best back woods. Playing the forehand, my intention in this position would be to trail the jack into the ditch for four. If this intention does not work out, my wood would certainly remove at least one or two of O's offending woods. The worst that could happen would be to lose two shots.

A common type of position where no element of luck is involved and X's skip stands or falls by his skill, touch and strength alone is shown in Figure 12. There is no room on the backhand for a firing shot, so X's skip must simply play the straightforward forehand draw to the best of his ability. At the top of his form he may draw the shot, but as consistency is such an important part of bowls, he must always draw well enough to obtain second or, at worst, third shot.

5 Playing the Percentages

Winning bowls is all about playing the percentages. There is a time to take a risk and a time not to. You will consider, of course, the score, the number of ends played, or, in the case of a team match, the overall position, but there are certain situations in which one should almost always take a risk or otherwise.

In Figure 13, player O holds three shots. Player X, about to bowl his last wood, has no possible means of drawing to the jack. He elects to fire, as shown, at wood A. If he hits it at a slight angle, woods B and D could be taken out which would still leave C as the shot wood, but in all probability that would be the only score.

If, in firing, the jack was taken through to the three back woods, it would probably leave player O with these three shots but at least, from player X's point of view, this is no worse than it was before.

In short, barring an exceptional stroke of luck, player X is bound to concede at least one shot but − again barring exceptional bad luck − he is unlikely to concede more than the three he is already down. In these circumstances, this is a risk worth taking.

In Figure 14, though, caution must be the watchword. Player X holds one shot but he has three quite useful woods at the back. Player O, with his last wood, dare not be heavy handed. If he is, a glancing contact on either X's shot wood or the jack will take the jack into X's other three woods at the back. If this happens, O concedes three shots instead of one. In this situation, player O should attempt to draw dead weight to the jack. If he bowls an exceptionally good wood, he may get the shot; if he does not, at least he is sure of conceding only one.

There are many occasions, too, when one side may hold the initiative and there is a choice between a positive shot, which

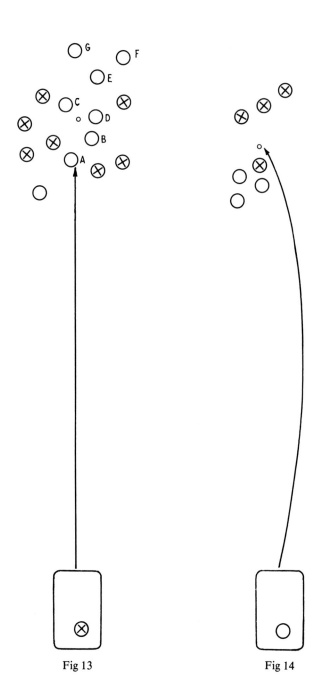

Fig 13

Fig 14

could lead to a five or six shot count, or a careful, consolidating type of shot which will make one or two shots a near certainty. Your choice here will often depend on what sort of player, even what sort of character, you are. Are you a bit of a gambler, prepared to lose £1 or win a £1? Or are you quite happy with 20p if this means you really can't lose more than 20p?

The more precise you are in judging the strength at which your wood reaches the head, the easier it is to foresee the range of possibilities. If you bowl only at dead weight, the number of bowls you will disturb is very limited. However, playing with an extra yard of weight or slightly more, even the most far-sighted player can be surprised by how things turn out. The greater the strength, the more serious a slight inaccuracy may be and the more possibility there is of good or bad luck.

The pessimist always expects bad luck rather than good and therefore tends to bowl dead weight and keep the game tight to keep luck out of the game as much as he can. The optimist, knowing that as long as he does not take foolish risks he will have his share of good luck as well as bad, tends to adopt a freer approach. He also has an advantage over the pessimist in that when the latter is forced to chance his arm – as everyone is sometimes – he will tend not to approach the situation with much confidence and will often be committed to delivering a bad wood before it has even left his hand.

However scientific and skilful you are, you can never take luck out of the game, though there is a world of difference between pure luck – like a punter sticking a pin in a list of runners – and giving yourself the best chance, like a student of form who can weigh up the various factors and make his selection without too much emotion or wishful thinking. There is another psychological factor about luck: if you can get your opponent thinking that the luck is running your way (even though, in reality, you may have chosen certain shots which appear to have given you some luck) he may lose heart. If he gets the feeling that the gods are against him, or that it isn't his day, you are at a tremendous advantage.

It is often a great test of character for a player to endure a run of bad luck. Some give in to it – almost start looking for it – others react by trying all the harder. I always try to be in the second category, though there are still occasions when, however hard you try, a stroke of luck seems to turn a match.

I well remember the semi-final of the EBA Fours against Burton House, Lincolnshire at Mortlake in 1972. It was an unusual opening. We scored five on the first end only to drop five on the second and another two on the third. With my last wood as skip on the fourth end, I had a chance to trail the jack for an eight (Figure 15). Our opponents held two shots but, taking a forehand arc, my last wood curled in perfectly to catch the jack full in the face.

'You've got it,' shouted the rest of my four, but almost before the words were out of their mouths the jack (which, of course, is much lighter than the woods) sprang back off that wood and rebounded to give them four shots instead of the eight we would have had.

So instead of being six in front, we were six behind and, hard as we tried, we never got over it. We lost 25–12 and Burton House went on to win the championship.

Another end which sticks in my mind is one in the 1977 EBA Triples Championship quarter-final when we were one up with five ends to play (Figure 16). Bowling as O, we already lay one shot and I could have tried to draw another for two. On the other hand, by trailing the jack into our five back woods, there was a chance of a five or six, which would have given us a commanding lead of six or seven.

Unfortunately, I was a fraction out and instead of my wood catching the jack flush it caught it half-ball to send it to the left, as shown, to give our opponents two shots.

Nevertheless, confronted by this position again I would still choose to go for the six because the odds were in my favour. If, for instance, I had caught the jack half-ball the other side, it would still have carried to my five back woods for five and if I had missed the jack altogether I would still have scored the one I held.

56

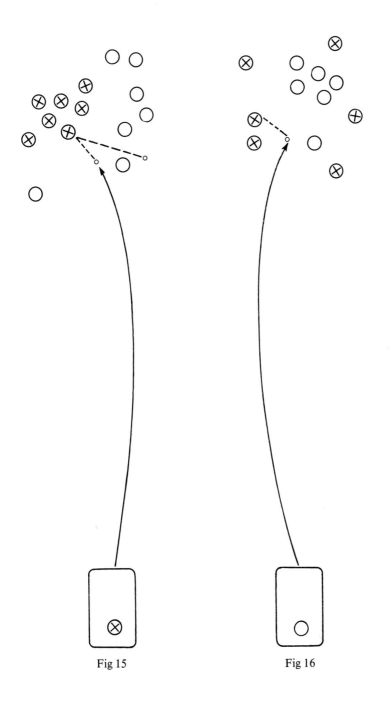

Fig 15

Fig 16

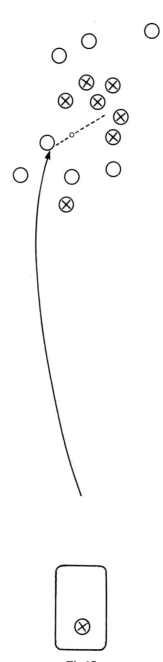

Fig 17

I'll end this section by recalling an occasion when I went for a big count and got it. It was in a Middleton Cup match against Warwickshire in 1977. We were 2–9 down after six ends and struggling. They lay shot on the seventh end (Figure 17), but my last wood took out their shot wood with about a half-ball contact and trailed the jack into our cluster of woods for seven.

I enjoy a tight game – a single to one side, a single to the other and so on – and at top level many matches are like that. But the spice or thrill of the game to my mind is the variety of shots, the way a situation changes several times in the same end with first one side and then the other holding the advantage.

To look at it from another angle, if both sides are bowling a tight sort of game, things can settle into a fairly predictable pattern. But if you can get your opponent(s) wondering what you might do, or better still, a little nervous of you, then you will have that mental advantage which is so important.

Shots can always go wrong, of course, and there are times when anything other than caution would be foolish, but in general I like to play as positively as I can. It gives me more enjoyment than playing a more limited game.

Of course, if it should happen that the other members of my rink have bowled their hearts out to give me, as skip, a one or two shot advantage and I, trying to make this four or five, have given our advantage away, I would naturally think twice about again attempting a shot with an element of risk if there was a reasonable alternative. Not only would my own confidence tend to be somewhat affected, but – and perhaps more to the point – there would be the danger of my lead, No2 or No3 losing heart if their good play was coming to nothing.

A skip should have confidence in the other members of his Four but it is even more important that they should have confidence in their skip.

One thing which strikes me about these diagrams is how much easier the situations look on paper than they do on the green. To execute such shots successfully needs the precise control of line, length and touch, which comes only through years of practice and experience. There is no substitute for skill; looking at these diagrams won't automatically make you a better player, but it should give you some insight into the range of shots that are available when the head lies in a certain way.

6 Last Ditch Efforts

By far the most important part of a bowling green is, of course, its beautifully level expanse of grass but, surrounding it, is a ditch which is also, in a sense, part of the playing area. Ditches used to vary a great deal. The width has always been standardised, at between 8 and 15in, but until the EBA introduced legislation insisting that ditches on all new greens must be cut $1\frac{1}{2}$in deep below the playing surface, some were shallow and some were deep.

Ditches on many old greens still do not conform to the new standard – although some clubs have carried out alterations – but on championship greens the standard measurement is religiously observed.

When the jack to be trailed is in a $1\frac{1}{2}$in deep ditch, the bowler can still see its position from the mat. If it lay in a deeper ditch, he could not see it and would therefore have to bowl, in a championship, to a white marker or, in a less important match, to a handkerchief placed above the jack on the bank.

On the other hand, if the ditch is not deep enough a wood could steeplechase over the top of the jack – using it like a ramp – and bounce back on to the green.

The new regulations, in fact, stipulate that the bank should be raised a minimum of 9in from the green's playing surface, which should ensure that no wood which hits the bank will return into play. Such a regulation would, incidentally, have made a freak shot which I made in the 1970 Denny Cup Final against Richmond impossible – and quite right too.

We led 21–1 after four ends, trailed 23–25 after ten, led 43–31 after fifteen but started the last end five down.

On the Rink where I was skip, we were two down and in such a position (Figure 18) that the only course was to fire and hope for the best. My wood crashed into the jack with such force that it hit the bank and bounded back to leave us lying two shots to the good. With my remaining wood I made it three. Our other skip, Graham Harrison, needing two shots to draw and three to win, held three when his opposing skip, Fred Mortimore, fired but in so doing, gave us an extra shot to leave us winners by two.

My own club, Vines Park, has recently built a new green and Worcestershire's county officials were meticulous in inspecting it at various stages of construction. Ironically, they could only be concerned initially with ditches and banks as the playing surface itself needs time to settle and inevitably further work to iron out untrue running, as much as is ever possible. As far as selecting a green for important matches is concerned, the only test which can be applied is how it plays.

Any wood which runs into the ditch without trailing the jack is a 'dead' wood and is removed from play, but any wood which, when it is initially bowled, touches the jack, before or after contacting other woods, or striking the jack alone, is designated a 'toucher' and remains in play even if it should continue into the ditch or be subsequently struck there. All touchers are marked with chalk when that particular shot comes to rest in order to avoid potential confusion over which wood was or was not a toucher.

A perfect shot is to trail the jack into the ditch in such a way that the wood remains touching it; such a shot cannot be beaten and rarely occurs, but it is not unheard of for a jack to be trailed into the ditch with a full contact and the wood to remain touching it, particularly if it is near the ditch to start with.

The deciding end of the 1977 Worcestershire Pairs Championship finished with the jack in the ditch (Figure 19). Clive Hall and Tony Russell, who had won the EBA title at Worthing the previous week, bowling X, lay game but their opposing skip, Alan Day, bowling O, decided, if he could, to trail the jack into the ditch. He did so, but only with a glancing contact so that instead of the wood following the jack, they went in opposite directions.

Day's wood, a toucher, now lay shot 5ft from the jack in the ditch. He also now lay game. Russell therefore had to play a wide

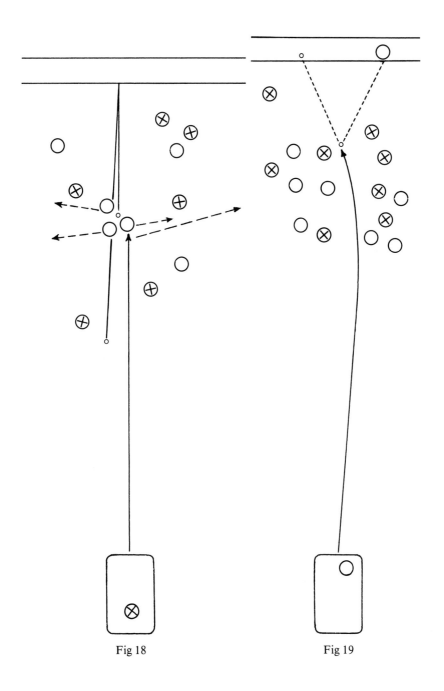

Fig 18   Fig 19

backhand draw to get within 5ft of the jack, without going into the ditch. For a bowler of his class this was not particularly difficult although it was more difficult than it would have been if the jack had been on the green because he would then have been bowling to a 5ft radius rather than a 5ft half-radius. There was also the added pressure of the result depending on that one shot. As it happened, though, he managed it comfortably and bowled his wood 3ft short of the ditch for the shot he needed.

The ditch played an important part in our victory over Australia in the 1976 World Championship Triples when we were two shots down on the last end and scored three to win. This, in fact, helped us win the Silver Medal.

The position was that, with the jack only 18in from the ditch, Australia held two shots (Figure 20). Our skip, Tom Armstrong, had two woods to come. The head was too congested to draw the shot – and in any case one shot was not enough – so with his last-but-one wood he knocked one of Australia's scoring woods into the ditch and with his last wood did the same to the other. In both cases, a full contact had to be made on the opposing wood to prevent our wood going in the ditch as well and thus, because it had not touched the jack, out of play. Tommy judged both perfectly and his woods remained where Australia's scoring woods had been for our winning three.

It is more common in this type of situation to see an attempt to 'burn up the end'. If one side can see no other possibility of retrieving a losing position on a certain end, one of them – probably the skip – will fire with the intention of sending the jack into the ditch, not by striking it with his own wood but knocking other woods in the head on to it. If the jack finishes in the ditch or leaves the rink across the string (ie out of play sideways) that end does not count and is replayed.

Any wood which goes over the string, even in the ditch, is out of play. An example of this came in an end I shall always remember from our match against South Africa in the World Championship Triples. It is almost the only occasion I can think of where the pyschological crux of the match occurred on the very first end.

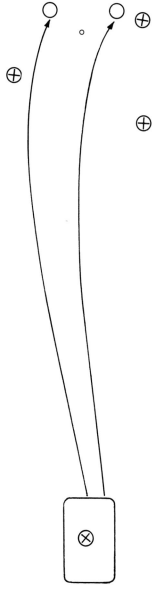

Fig 20

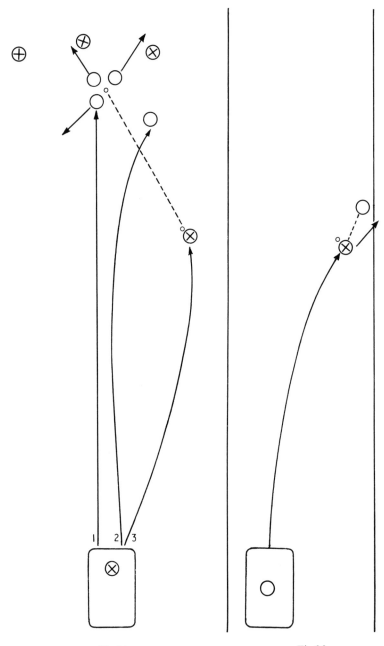

Fig 21

Fig 22

Kevin Campbell, the South African lead, bowled three perfect woods – all about 3in from the jack. A fourth similar wood would have hidden the jack completely (Figure 21).

Our lead, David Bryant, who had put his first two woods round the back, conferred with me, and even at this early stage, to forestall South Africa putting us in an impossible position, decided to fire in order to open up the head. It is very unusual for a lead to fire but the alternative – waiting for me to fire with my first wood – was akin to me wasting my first delivery.

He caught their front wood right on the button. The force of the shot caused the jack to rebound at a diagonal. It finished only a couple of feet from the string.

Their No2's first wood finished about 5ft from the jack. Playing No2 for us, I then bowled a toucher. Their No2 caught my wood from the backhand and sent it over the string (Figure 22) while sending the jack up the green. But with my next wood I bowled another toucher and we ended up scoring four shots on this end.

I think our opponents must have felt that they had produced the perfect opening and still had nothing to show for it. We, of course, were delighted that we had managed to turn the tables and, full of confidence, we went on to win 25–12.

67

7   The Television Age

Over the last five years, bowls has gradually become recognised as a television sport. A game ordinarily takes too long to show in its entirety but both shortened games and edited highlights have come across without loss of atmosphere or authenticity. Singles has been the form of the game most favoured not only because it is easy to dramatise but because there are simply less bodies to get in the way of the cameras.

Edited versions of the EBA Singles finals have been shown for the last few years on BBC 1's Grandstand; BBC Scotland produced an excellent four man knock-out which David Bryant won in early 1978; and BBC Northern Ireland recorded a similar series for showing later that year, though the unavailability of editing facilities, which made it necessary for games to be decided on an artificial 25 minutes' time limit, was an unsatisfactory feature.

The great television breakthrough came with the Kodak Masters on BBC 2 which was transmitted in September 1978, a series which could well achieve the mass exposure for bowls that Pot Black achieved for snooker.

My mind goes back, though, to the first television bowls tournament, the National Benzole Master Bowler event which was recorded in HTV's studios in Cardiff. Because we were in a studio, the green could only be 50ft long instead of the usual 35–40yd and there was a line instead of a ditch. The green, particularly after the lights had warmed it up, was lightning fast and the speed of delivery had to be judged very delicately indeed.

There were two players for each of the home countries but the final was an all-England one between David Bryant and myself. It was one of the most exciting matches I have ever played and through the good offices of HTV and Richard Watts, a Cardiff

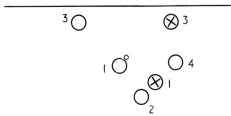

Fig 23

bowls enthusiast who originated the series, I recently had the pleasure of viewing the match at leisure and making notes on its development and its climax. In the series of figures, I am bowling O and my opponent X.

David led 5–1 after three ends and 7–4 after six before I made it 6–7. At the eighth end (see Fig 23), trying to bowl the jack to maximum length, I sent it in the ditch. The jack reverted to David but I delivered a toucher with my first wood. His first wood was also a good one but I strengthened my position with another goodish wood, not quite good enough for second shot but half-blocking his forehand approach.

David's second wood was a shade too heavy and finished in the ditch or rather, as I have explained, across the line. For the purposes of this tournament, any woods which crossed the lines were 'dead' and could not count – though as we saw in the last chapter they can often be useful under the usual rules.

My third wood gave me some useful back position as some insurance against the possibility of David trailing the jack through. This led to him choosing to attempt to knock his first wood in at just the weight to reach the jack and jar my first wood away. He took too much green and finished wide but as this gave him a new and slightly easier option with his last wood of taking the backhand to strike my first wood and send the jack across to his third wood my position was by no means safe.

It was also obvious that I had to be very careful with my last wood. The last thing I wanted to do was knock his first wood in for shot so with this wood I was much less concerned with trying to draw another shot than with trying to make the position more difficult for David.

Ideally, I would have liked to place my last wood between the jack and his third, thus eliminating the new option the latter had created. I was a little short but David was wide and heavy with his last wood as he tried to knock the jack towards his third. I was quite happy with the single which brought me to 8–8.

On the ninth end (see Fig 24), to a full-length jack within a yard of the ditch, I delivered my first three woods to within 18in of the

Fig 24

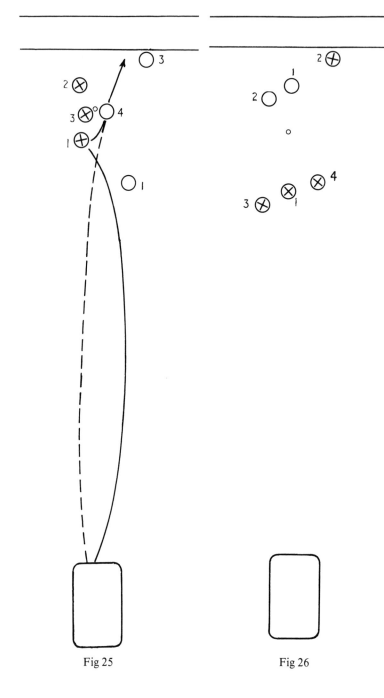

Fig 25   Fig 26

target which, though I say it myself, was not bad going in those fast conditions, while David put each of his first three woods in the ditch. I can't think that he has ever done this before or since!

Just to show how easy it was to do this, I put my last in the ditch so, as he came to the mat with the last wood of the end there was the unusual sight of only three of the seven woods, all mine, remaining on the green.

He made the best of a bad job and drew third shot but the other two shots gave me a 9–7 lead with which to start the tenth of the scheduled eleven ends. Another shot here and I would have been virtually home and dry with David needing a four on the last end, but he showed what a marvellous pressure player he is by taking a four.

After I had been 4ft short with my first (see Fig 25) he took the initiative by putting his first only 9in or so in front of the jack.

My second went in the ditch so when David put his second again only 9in from the jack, this time at the back, he was starting to look dangerous. Things looked even worse when I tried to trail the jack but I went through and he tightened the net with a toucher which finished only 6 or 7in from the jack. Although he lay three shots, I thought I was still in with a chance when I sent up a good wood which, after a cannon, was either shot or second shot. I would have been happy with either but David's last wood was perfect and, as the dotted line shows, took out my shot wood to leave him with four shots.

After a reversal of fortune like that, from two up to two down, I remember getting that awful sinking feeling which comes over you when you can sense that your chance has gone. Of course, I tried to take no notice of it and battle on – as you must – but this kind of situation is a test of anyone's temperament. There is also a special pressure involved in playing David, not just because he's such a good player, but because he has won so many big tournaments and his reputation stands so high that it's very difficult to regard him as just another opponent. In the circumstances, on the eleventh and last end (see Fig 26), I felt I did very well to get a two and thus force the match to an extra end.

David's first was 15in from the jack but in front; mine was just shot at the back so when I drew a second shot with my second (his second having gone to the back) I was in the driving seat. His third wood cannoned his first wood and stayed in front of the jack. I therefore had a chance to draw another shot but was just a little too vigorous with my third wood and put it in the ditch.

I expected David's last wood to be a good one but, to my surprise, he was short again: I still held two shots. But, short as it was, that last wood cramped my attempt to draw the third shot which would have won me the match.

All too clearly I could see that, if my last wood was on the narrow side, it was quite on the cards that it could knock one of David's woods in for shot and thus give him the match.

Determined that my last wood would not be narrow, I took too much green and was also a shade too heavy. Even though this finished in the ditch, I was quite happy to have forced the extra end.

Winning the toss, I had no hesitation in giving the jack away, as any good class bowler, in these circumstances, likes to be in the position of delivering the last wood.

After his great four on the tenth end, David had bowled a shade more loosely on the eleventh but his first wood on this extra end (see Fig 27) was, looking at it from his point of view, a beauty: not only a toucher but one which forced me on to the bad hand, in this direction the forehand.

Attempting to trail, I put my first wood through the back of the green. David's second finished right alongside it, not a good position for me as, even if I did manage to trail the jack I could just as easily trail it to his back wood as mine.

Anyway, my second wood missed the target and finished in the ditch and David, with his third wood, made things look even darker for me with a short blocking wood which prevented me, with my third wood, having another try at what I had tried to do with my second.

I therefore decided to give it a little more weight to go inside his blocking wood and play on to his shot wood. I just missed it.

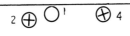

Fig 27

David's last wood just about tied up the match as, by putting it at the back of the green to cover my back wood, I no longer had the option of coming into his shot wood and sending the jack to the right of my back wood for shot.

I had some sort of shot on but David's blocker at the front and two back woods meant that I had no margin for error. I attempted to trail the jack gently in the hope of getting shot with that wood. It was very difficult and my last wood just failed to get past David's blocker.

I had lost, but it was such a great match that I didn't mind too much. I also firmly believe that the entertainment value of this match paved the way for selling bowls, not only again to HTV but to other television companies.

Postscript

I wrote the last chapter just before leaving for the Commonwealth Games, of which bowls has long been an established part, in Edmonton. But perhaps of more long-term significance from the game's point of view are the efforts which are being made to bring European nations, where bowls has previously been unknown, into the bowling fraternity.

David Bryant, Bill Denny, a bowls enthusiast whose father donated the Denny Cup, Donald Newby, editor of *World Bowls*, and Bill Walker, Managing Director of the Teesside Indoor Bowling Centre, are the principals of an export company whose aim is to sell the game of bowls to other countries within the EEC. The company lays greens, either grass outdoors or carpet indoors, and sells equipment, the primary concern being a desire on the part of the principals to see the game prosper and expand. From such efforts as this, I believe that one day we could see bowls in the Olympic Games.

Meanwhile, thousands will continue to play at their own various standards for enjoyment and sociability and that, for me, will always be what bowls is about.

This book was intended to impart a few insights into how to improve your game and how top players think but improvement comes in the end not through reading books but by putting what you've read into practice, so get out there and play!